Blockchain

The Key to Learning and Understanding Blockchain and How It Relates to Bitcoin, Cryptocurrency, and Mining

Roger Bray

© **Copyright 2017 by Roger Bray - All rights reserved.**

The following eBook is reproduced below with the goal of providing information that is as accurate and as reliable as possible. Regardless, purchasing this eBook can be seen as consent to the fact that both the publisher and the author of this book are in no way experts on the topics discussed within, and that any recommendations or suggestions made herein are for entertainment purposes only. Professionals should be consulted as needed before undertaking any of the action endorsed herein.

This declaration is deemed fair and valid by both the American Bar Association and the Committee of Publishers Association and is legally binding throughout the United States.

Furthermore, the transmission, duplication or reproduction of any of the following work, including precise information, will be considered an illegal act, irrespective whether it is done electronically or in print. The legality extends to creating a secondary or tertiary copy of the work or a recorded copy and is only allowed with an express written consent of the Publisher. All additional rights are reserved.

The information in the following pages is broadly considered to be a truthful and accurate account of facts, and as such any inattention, use or misuse of the information in question by the reader will render any resulting actions solely under their purview. There are no scenarios in which the publisher or the original author of this work can be in any fashion deemed liable for any hardship or damages that may befall them after undertaking information described herein.

Additionally, the information found on the following pages is intended for informational purposes only and should thus be considered, universal. As befitting its nature, the information presented is without assurance regarding its continued validity or interim quality. Trademarks that mentioned are done without written consent and can in no way be considered an endorsement from the trademark holder.

Table of Contents

Introduction 1

The Basics 4

Blockchain Uses 10

History 28

Cryptocurrency and Blockchain 33

How to Use Blockchain 42

Pros and Cons 62

Conclusion 71

Introduction

Congratulations on purchasing your personal copy of Blockchain: The Key to Learning and Understanding Blockchain and How It Relates to Bitcoin, Cryptocurrency, and Mining. Thank you for doing so.

The following chapters will provide you strategies and tips on how you can use blockchain technology to improve your digital business, not only with finances but in many other areas as well.

The following chapters will provide you with a short history of blockchain as well as its uses. The blockchain is the perfect technology for people that have a business, especially if you have a strong online presence. Simply put, blockchain is a tracking system for digital transactions among several other things.

In the past several years, blockchain has become increasingly popular with the media. While not criticism-free, people have claimed that it's nothing more than a shared database that venture capitalist have hyped up, it truly is a technology that could cause great societal, economic, and social change.

For the most part, blockchain has been using a financial service tool that is used to upgrade its efficiency and transparency, as well as reducing the cost. This has made blockchain so popular that its technology is used all around the world either by innovation labs or independently run by banks and other types of entities. Many start-ups have been experimenting with different types of applications that could use blockchain technology and trying to use it to figure out problems in the financial world.

The United States and Western Europe has shown the most excitement for blockchain technology. Their discussions about it tend to be about region-specific perspectives and problems. The biggest problem that the technology has had for its spread is different entities being able to collaborate with other entities. This could be commercial, financial, and government companies and entities.

With the information housed within this book, I hope that I can provide readers a deeper and better understanding of blockchain. Maybe if we can spread more knowledge about this amazing technology, more people will begin to use it. You will also learn that it no longer has to be used just for the financial industry, and it can be very helpful in pretty much any area of business.

The blockchain is the most useful when it can have multiple implementations where many people are about to benefit from it. The blockchain is more challenging in a collaborative way than it is technical. But this also is not only a problem for blockchain, and it a common problem that is faced by many other technologies.

There are plenty of books on this subject on the market, thanks again for choosing this one! Every effort was made to ensure it is full of as much useful information as possible. Please enjoy!

The Basics

Blockchain was created for one purpose. That purpose was to agree with who has ownership over different balances. It is basically a tracking device.

When someone makes an online transaction like paying a person with bitcoin, a message gets created that has three components; a record showing proof of available funds from the buyer, the wallet's address of the recipient, and how much they are going to get paid. If there are other conditions that the buyer has specified, those are stated, and the buyer's signature is marked on the message. Digital signatures are composed of private and public code; the message gets encrypted with a code that is private and sent on for verification. The buyer's public code is what is used to decrypt the message.

This process is used so that double spend will not happen. This is a huge risk with digital currency. Double spend is when Bonnie gives Jane a dollar and then gives Dean that same dollar. This might not seem right with our current banking system, and it's true that if Bonnie were giving a true dollar to Dean and Jane, that she wouldn't be able to double spend. With digital currency, it's just data. Anyone can edit or copy the information, and this makes it possible for anyone to give money away that they do not really have. If anyone could actually get away with doing that, it would cause a breakdown in the trust of the network.

A block will take about ten minutes to validate. This is why some buyers add tips to help speed the process up and encourage people to validate their request.

Since anybody could check a change against a ledger and get it validates, a blockchain gets rid of the need for a centralized entity like banks to manage information. By eliminating third parties, it will help save on transaction fees, processing times, and limits how large a transaction can be and to whom it may be sent.

Basically, blockchain is a database that keeps a continuously growing list of records called block, that are secured from revisions and changes. Each block contains a timestamp and lint to the block before it.

Non-Technological Explanation

Let's see if I can break this down without using all the fancy modern terms. Let's explain it like blockchain was set in pre-electricity times.

This village does not have centralized currency. They only use the barter system. The villagers get angry with how inefficient the bartering system is. They do not understand a central banking currency and worry about it. They finally decide to use a decentralized account system and write all the transactions down in a public ledger.

When someone decides to give money to someone else, they write down who they are, who the recipient is, the amount they are giving them, and the date on a piece of paper. They send it to a secure box to be written in the ledger. Keepers of the ledger then process all the submitted transactions. Several keepers must sign off on transactions before they are put into the ledger to get rid of any mistakes and fraud. With every transaction, a certain amount is put aside to give the keepers to make sure the important transactions are entered first.

When the transactions are agreed upon by all the keepers, they are written down on scrolls and then encased in glass. These are called blocks. In every block, there is a shortened version of the transaction. Every one of the blocks is chained together and put into the public archives. This makes all the transactions permanent, and the public can see them.

This is the simplest way to look at how blockchain works. It is not as complicated as some make it seem to be.

Understanding Blockchain

Blockchain technology is fairly new. This means there are many different ways to learn the system and terminology that hasn't been standardized yet. Blockchain works as a shared, append-only, replicated database where the access is shared with other participants, and everybody does validation. The most common elements of blockchain are:

There is data storage that usually holds the financial transactions but really can hold any type of data. There is data replication on different systems in real time. Blockchain has a peer to peer network instead of a hierarchical model. Digital signature and cryptography is used to help prove identity, authenticity, and enforce access rights. Blockchain also has structures that cause record changes to be hard. If someone were to try, it is easily detectable.

Blockchains are different in how they function as to whether they are public or private. If the network is public, more security is in place than there needs to be with a private network. Blockchains have differing protocols that depend on if anybody has to write them or if the participants must be limited. The blockchain's desire affects the engineering system directly. Public blockchains are more secure than private.

The blockchain is just a file. It is a data structure. It is how data is put together logically and stored. Other types of data structures are text files; comma separated values, images, lists, and databases. A blockchain is similar to a database.

The blocks within the chain are like pages in a book. The book's pages contain a story and information about it like title, page number, and chapter. This type of data about data is referred to as meta-data.

With blockchain, every block contains the contents of a bitcoin transaction along with a header. The header is the information about the block.

Every block is then placed in an ordered fashion so that anyone will know the chain's order. For example, the pages in a book are all numbered, so if you were to rip them all out and shuffle them up, you could still put the book back in order. Just like a page, each block references back to another block with its own unique fingerprint. This fingerprint is determined by the block's content.

Blockchain Uses

Blockchain has shown it is a revolutionary tool used in the financial industry. This is very true with bitcoin. Blockchain can be used to help improve other industries, too.

Not for Finance Only

The blockchain is usually only spoken about in conjunction to bitcoin. Many people do not realize that blockchains can be used differently. The way it works provides extra security and more ease to many other areas of the digital business. Because the blockchain network is decentralized and transparent, it helps the development of non-refutable, unbreakable record of data. The first, non-financial, use in digital identity.

1. **Digital identity**

Digital security is a huge problem in the world today. There are people who can hack into accounts and get anyone's personal information from websites and thus steals their identity. Now, think about a world where you wouldn't have to worry about having your identity stolen. Blockchain makes this possible.

Blockchain technology makes efficient and secure tracking and helps to manage digital identities. This makes sign-ins seamless and easier and reduces fraud. It could help with banking, healthcare, national security, online retailing, and citizenship documentation. Identity authorization and authentication are intricately woven in culture and commerce all around the world.

If you can remember back to 2013 when Target had a data breach between November 27 and December 15, more than 70 million people had their information stolen. This information included their debit or credit card numbers, names, the credit cards expiration date, CVV, phone numbers, mailing addresses, and even their e-mail addresses.

Things like this data breach and hacked databases have been spotlighted on the numerous problems in a society that is based on advanced technology. It goes to show that the security in place right now is not doing a good job. People should not have to worry about someone getting their information.

Blockchain offers a solution to many digital identity issues. It has a way to uniquely authenticate in an immutable, safe, and secure manner. Most security solutions are problematic password-based systems.

Blockchain's authentication is controlled by an undeniable identity verification that uses a public key cryptography. With this authentication, checks are performed to decide if a transaction was signed with the right private key. It assumes the person using it has use of the private code and is the owner, making identity unimportant.

Ways you could use blockchain identity technology:

- IDs
- Passports
- Online Account Login
- E-Residency
- Birth Certificates
- Digital Identities
- Wedding Certificates

1. Distributed Cloud Storage

Data storage that uses blockchain will create a massive disrupt sometime in the future.

The current cloud storage providers are centralized. This means users have put all their trust in one single storage. These providers have control over all your online information.

With blockchain cloud storage, it becomes decentralized. The means you do not have to put all your trust in one entity to keep your information protected. There are some beginners who are beta testing blockchain cloud storage. These are slock.it, stori.io, and factom.com.

1. **Decentralized Notary**

The best and most fascinating feature of blockchain is the timestamp. The network confirms the state of one piece of data at a certain time. Since blockchain is trustless and a decentralized network, the timestamp confirms the life of a specific thing at a specific time. This would be provable in a court of law. Only a notary could do this in the past.

This works because a user would upload their file and pay a fee for the transaction to be cryptographically proven on the blockchain. The file will never be stored online, so there is not a risk of unapproved publication of anyone's information.

After the file is uploaded anonymously, and the fee is paid, a hash of the file will be created as a part of the transaction. This will use the ledger-like system and the public nature of the blockchain to house your documents as proof. This will allow the information to be verified if a problem arises about the authorship or dates. One website that offers this service is proofofexistence.com.

1. **Digital Voting**

The main problem with getting the electoral process online is due to security. With blockchain, a voter could check to see if their vote was sent successfully while keeping them anonymous to everyone else. The Liberal Alliance, a political party in Denmark, was the first to use blockchain voting. Voter turnout in America is still very low. If we could implement distributed digital voting, more non-voters might actually begin to vote.

In 2013, Estonia was the only country to run internet voting on a large scale. They had a team observe their process and witnessed officials using downloaded software instead of insecure internet connections. Norway decided to cancel e-voting for all their elections because voters feared that their votes would be public domain and might undermine the democratic process.

1. **Trading Ownership**

Ownership of all digital properties can be established in a person-to-person way with blockchain. Blockchains could be used to trade and establish ownership of absolutely anything that is available on the internet. This makes it possible to pre-sale tokens that show ownership of anything, and this includes merchandise, tickets, subscriptions, products, even the rights to other people's time. This way they can distribute, create, and then exchange on a platform that is supported.

Smart Contracts

Smart contracts are still rather new but are growing in popularity within the online industry. Many people are beginning to see the potential of smart contracts. They are being used in small amounts right now, but it is easy to see the benefits that smart contracts could have on a bigger scale. They could replace the need for lawyers since every detail and change is documented within the blockchain. This allows everything to get recorded. Because it is all automated, everything will stay up to date, and it is very unlikely that it could or would be tampered with.

It is still in the early stages and does not have many supporters. There is not any evidence of what it could do on a bigger scale but shows promise in peer to peer effectiveness. It is being said the smart contracts are a big breakthrough innovation from what the small interactions are showing.

Smart contracts play a huge part in the blockchain application. They can relieve many intangible benefits that technology today is missing. These contracts are activated when a command or program is completed. It is then housed in a block and becomes a part of the whole chain.

You might compare a smart contract to a debit card. A deduction is made from your account each time you use your card. Smart contracts work in a similar way except they are decentralized since the hard drive is located in different places around the world. It is a computer code that records how and when changes are made.

When smart contracts are finished on a public blockchain, third parties cannot stop this transaction. They get rid of needing third parties. They can execute by themselves without needing any middlemen. This makes them very secure. Due to the blockchain system, it is almost impossible to hack.

Remember, blockchains are public ledgers, so if a smart contract is made with a blockchain, it can be seen by anybody who has a copy of the chain. The will make the contract available to the public for viewing so no one can debate of the contents. It is just a digital reference of what happened. This is why they are looked at as either good or bad, depending on what the contract holds.

Here are some smart contracts:

- Financial

Cryptocurrency has made several different uses of smart contracts. Smart contracts can perform any action without needing third parties to hold up the rules. Smart contracts can translate binary code to commands so the system can perform. The system will then detect the highest bidder in the auction and then send them the item. Everybody else's money goes back to them. This is why smart contracts are so promising.

- Property Law

People can use cryptocurrencies like ether or bitcoin to trade assets using blockchains. Cryptographic technologies get used to making sure the owner of the digital coin is the only person who can spend it. This is like physical items that get embedded with microchips.

- Credit Enforcement

This is the extension of the property law. This is one-way smart contracts can be used in the real world. Smart contracts can shut down your account if you do not make your payments. If you cannot make your agreed upon payment on a credit card, and you have gone over your limit, your account gets disabled until you can make a payment.

- Breach Prevention

Smart contracts are helpful in the movie and music industry. Digital Rights Management helps to prevent people from unauthorized use of any video or music that is protected by copyright. A blockchain can track these copyrights for each music and video. Whenever the video or music is used, the copyright owner will receive royalty payments. The smart contract can set the terms of how a payment can be made between the producers, songwriters, and performers. Because everything is available in public blockchain, the will know it hasn't changed.

- Double Deposit

Some of the first uses of the double deposit were BlackHalo and BitHalo. The double deposit method was designed to be used in cryptocurrency trading. It works so that if two parties try to cheat each other out of money, they will both lose the exact same amount that they might have earned. It does not worry about figuring out who wasn't doing what they were supposed to; it just makes sure that both parties agree. If they cannot in a given amount of time, then both will get penalized. This gives both parties good reasons to be agreeable.

- Oracle Contracts

Smart contracts depend on data that is entered into the blockchain system. This makes it hard to tell what the real consequences are. Smart contracts might not be able to tell who is or is not telling the truth in any given situation. Oracle contracts were made to fix this. Oracles get information from external sources that is later used as a source data for smart contracts.

Smart Contracts VS Traditional Contracts

A traditional contract that is drawn up by legal professionals relies on third parties to uphold the terms of the contract. They are written in legal jargon and need huge amounts of paperwork. Traditional contracts take a significant amount of time, but they might also be debated. This vagueness is created because everyone does not understand the legal jargon that the contracts are written in. Professionals who write the contracts can enforce them as they want to. If the parties who are involved do not agree with the terms of the contract, or one part feels like the other violated the terms, then the matter will be resolved by the public judiciary system. If things are taken to court, then that will incur more expenses and time.

Computer programmers handle smart contracts by using smart contract tools and programs. These are totally digital. This means there is not any need for paperwork. Smart contracts are written in binary code, and the code tells what the terms and any consequences are. They are easier to understand since there is not much legal jargon and a third party is not required to uphold the contract.

Technical Mechanics and How They are Implemented

Let's go back to the blockchain for a moment. Earlier, you received a brief overview of what a blockchain is and how it works. Now that you have an understanding of it let's dig a bit deeper.

How They Work

Each time a node connects to a network for the very first time, it will download a complete copy of the blockchain database to your server or computer.

The node network controls the blockchain database. The nodes are an entry point for new data. These are also made by new data and validation that was submitted within the blockchain.

You might wonder how in a system that has no source of truth, the network can come to a consensus and agreement of what needs to be written in the blockchain. You might also wonder how conflicts get resolved when qualified people can contradict each other and there is not anyone to settle the dispute.

Protocols are the boss. A protocol is a predetermined rule that everyone has agreed on the business and technical validity of data, and it figures out how the consensus is reached.

A group of transactions that are similar makes up a block. Then the blocks get put together in chronological order and form a chain, hence the name blockchain. Nodes store the new block in a local blockchain database on a computer or server.

One solution to keeping the nodes acting on a time priority is keeping the first one and getting rid of the second. There is a slight chance that the message that was heard by other nodes might be heard in a different order. Messages can grow and parts of the network might hear that A happened but B hasn't, and the other part of the network might hear that B happened but A didn't. The network is very unstable.

How can you resolve this? Each node works based on its truth. The node that adds the next block makes its own version of events, and the other nodes see this and think that it is true.

There is a slight chance that within the network two different blocks might get attached to the chain at the same exact time by different nodes. This creates a fork in the chain. There is a consensus rule that helps the nodes figure out what block to believe. With bitcoin, their consensus rule is the longest chain. This means that the nodes believe the truth of both blocks and when another block is added to a forked block, then that block will become the truth. Now the longer chain is part of the actual blockchain.

Two pieces of conflicting data might be given to a node. One example is that A might say, "I give my shares to Richard," then B says, "I give all my share to Stacy." The node now needs to decide which one to keep and which one to reject since they cannot both logically coexist.

The broadest sense of a blockchain is a database that is spread out among different entities that are in sync. There is not a single controller. They are normally append-only. This means they can only be written and the data that it contains already cannot be changed. A user must get permission to change the data that is housed in the older blocks.

The blockchain has the potential to disturb the remittances platform since the opportunity to return value back to customers would be too much. Remittance platforms are both formal and informal. They can range from cash being sent across the country or world to friends and family to money transfer operators. These platforms are far from being foolproof and have many inefficiencies.

So, where does blockchain come in? A blockchain along with a digital wallet will allow a peer to peer transfers of digital currency almost instantly at little to no cost. Since the introduction of digital wallets that have currency conversion functions, it has opened the ability and opportunity for a safe and anonymous remittance of any currency. All the sender and receiver need to have is a smartphone with a digital wallet. Cost and features are set by the provider of the wallet.

Some people have concerns about remittances being made to fund terrorists or other illegal activities. This would make a wallet or ATM provider register with the right financial regulators and make their customer complete a security check before any transactions can take place. This is not hard to do as long as the right processes are built into the operating platform.

A blockchain is a tool that can help return charges to people that need them while leaving a healthy margin for wallet and ATM providers.

Ledgers

Any digital currency like bitcoin is a digital token that can be passed from user to user. The token does not have a tangible representation, this is why it is called an on-chain asset. It only exists on the blockchain, and having a token means nothing other than you claiming you own this token. It is uncertain as to what an on-chain assets role is in normal financial services. It will remain that way until it can be legally presented as real currency, shares, or other dematerialized assets.

Off-chain assets are on the other side of things. These are real-world items like currency, gold, or shares that can be digitally shown on a ledger by tokens provided by an issuer. This item will be kept safely by the issuer and then issue the digital token on a ledger against them. The token is a digital deed to the asset and can be given to other users.

Eventually, the user will give the digital token back to the issuer and make an offer on the real item. The idea is for blockchain asset ledgers to make the settlement for off chain assets faster and more efficient.

Events could also be recorded inside a blockchain. The event might be any kind of data and can be recorded for everyone to see it could be encrypted. Events could be messages between users, documents, shareholder votes, meeting minutes, industry agreed holidays, counterparty data, and much, much more. The blockchain adds one more level of protection since when the data is entered, it cannot be changed, has a timestamp, and this can be done without the added expense of a third party.

The Obstacles

With anything digital, blockchains have hurdles that must be overcome. Blockchains are most valuable when information is shared through national borders. This is also hard to achieve without a lot of political will and a group effort from all involved.

Usually, in organizations, businesses or governments, the ability to change already written data is something they do not want to get rid of. Complete transparency is a double-edged sword. Changes might be demanded here from either the grassroots demanding data be put on a blockchain to make it a record that cannot be edited. They might come from policymakers and regulators demanding these changes.

Blockchains aren't just about transparency. They could be used in industry platforms to share data that might be helpful to the whole company. The majority of players in the industry must come together to decide on what the platform needs to look like, who is going to pay for it, and what every participant will get. This will not be done in a day, nor is it cheap.

Switching technologies does cost money. There are old and inadequate legacy systems that are commonplace in most banks. The benefit and cost of replacing these systems just do not make sense to the bank. Blockchains must have clear business cases before banks even begin to adopt them.

History

Many people think blockchain and bitcoin are the same when in fact they are not. Blockchain has made its own history outside of bitcoin now. This is not saying it is not important to learn about the history of bitcoin while learning about blockchain since it is safe to say without bitcoin there wouldn't be a blockchain, at least not any mainstream knowledge.

Blockchain and Bitcoin

The original and widely known blockchain was the bitcoin blockchain. It works to show how blockchain technology works. The bitcoin blockchain is on thousands of computers around the world as a database file. Each copy is kept in order by the rules in the bitcoin protocol. This blockchain file contains a list of all the bitcoin transactions that ever happened since bitcoin launched. The ledger holds every record for bitcoin since January 2009.

The bitcoin blockchain is a permissionless database. This just means that anyone can write entries into the database without having to sign up, login, or ask permission from anyone in charge. To do this is you need to download opensource software and run it. This connects your computer to the internet with another computer that is running similar software. This software allows you to send and receive bitcoin data to others. You can also add more data to the blockchain.

A person can tell what account has how many bitcoins, who is sending them and to whom they are sending them. The transparency allows for people who validate to figure out if the transaction is legit or not. The can keep others from paying someone else with bitcoins that do not really exist.

Different Blockchains

There are thousands of blockchains, both private and public, running right now, but many of them do not have enough uptake. Ripple, NXT, and Ethereum have gained popularity as public systems built by blockchain technology. There are more that are currently being constructed as the blockchain industry begins to take shape.

Ripple

Ripple is between a public and private platform. They rely on validating nodes that are controlled by Ripple, Inc. They hope to dematerialize currencies and assets. Customers give actual assets to guardians that are called ripple gateways. These gateways then give the customer a token for these assets. This is similar to how goldsmiths used to issue receipts for gold deposits. These tokens are then sent to anyone who has a Ripple account. These can be traded for other tokens and then redeemed by giving the token back to the guardian for the actual asset.

NXT

This is a public platform; NXT genesis was made in November of 2013. It works a bit differently from bitcoin's blockchain. NXT uses a block called proof-of-stake as opposed to bitcoin's proof-of-work. Proof-of-stake gives rewards according to the amount of money you have in your account, instead of how much power you have used. NXT platforms can do more than just sending tokens. You could also message, token create, asset creation, decentralized exchange, and a marketplace.

Ethereum

This is a public platform that takes distributed computing to a whole new step. It acts as a giant consensus machine instead of a database. Its computations are Turing-complete, this means it can calculate whatever other computers can calculate, just a bit slower. Ethereum's genesis was started in July of 2015. It is the leading platform for permissionless smart contracts.

Importance

Blockchain has brought a revolutionary way to protect different transactions online. This will include any combination of the following:

- Replicated on a number of systems
- Financial transactions
- Has cryptography and digital signatures to help prove identities
- Exist on peer to peer networks
- Certain participants can read blockchain
- Certain participants can write blockchain
- It is hard to change historical records

What makes blockchain important and revolutionary? Blockchain will allow people to exchange digital assets anonymously. Blockchain will work for most types of transactions that involve a value. This might be money, goods, or property. Its uses are limitless. It could even be used for collecting taxes. It could help migrants send money to their family when banks make it difficult.

Blockchain also reduces fraud due to all transactions being recorded on a public ledger that everyone sees.

People use bitcoin and blockchain together, but blockchain can be used alone. It moves power from large entities, like banks to normal people. This makes it fast, safe, and cheap even if you do not know the people you are dealing with. Computers do all the validating using sophisticated algorithms to certify the exchange and record all the activity. Computers that are part of the network that processes the transactions are located all over the world. Most importantly they are not independently owned and operated. This processing is in real time and has better security than relying on a central authority.

Cryptocurrency and Blockchain

We have discovered that, even though it is more slow gong that some fintech people hoped for, alternative payment options, mainly mobile, are starting to gain more traction and are complementing the still dominate use of cash, by giving the consumers more convenience and choice in the way that they can access their money. The most frustrating and fascinating thing about alternative payments is how complex it can seem; so in this chapter, I am going to try and demystify a few common words that pop up a lot: cryptocurrencies and blockchain.

Cryptocurrency

Try and look at cryptocurrencies like a digital version of a regular fiat currency, something that the government has made a legal tender, but does not have the backing of a physical commodity. But where a fiat currency used to have a link with precious mineral values, a cryptocurrency causes scarcity through the complex world of digitally solving equations or mining to make a new token.

Every different cryptocurrency has their own claims that they can solve a problem or fill a role in a better way than any other solution which came before it. The factor that unifies all cryptocurrencies is the blockchain concept, and its knack for establishing ownership and identity of record transactions and the use of the enforcing "smart contracts."

The definition of cryptocurrency, as provided by Cryptocoins News, is, "a medium of exchange like normal currencies such as USD, but designed to exchange digital information through a process made possible by certain principles of cryptography. Cryptography is used to secure the transactions and to control the creation of new coins." A different way to describe it is that cryptocurrency is a type of electricity that is converted by solving equations so that you can create digital value units that can be used a form of payment. In the very simplest of definitions, cryptocurrency is a type of digital currency that, instead of being printed, is mined.

At the moment, the collective value of all cryptocurrencies is around $150 to $200 billion, their numbers fluctuate a lot, and so a lot of money is involved. There are a lot of people out that believe this is only the beginning. As the infrastructure and technology of these coins start to grow, cryptocurrencies that can provide a real and helpful solution to different problems may end up finding their self-increasing in value rapidly, just like bitcoin did. This means investors will find them extremely attractive.

But there is a big problem. A large amount of those more than 2,000 tokens and currencies do not have a real-world use or an opportunity of being picked up mainstream. This probably the reason why raising money with cryptocurrencies, ICOs, in China, is now illegal. A lot of governments, mostly in the West, aren't as eager to heavy hand their regulations.

This has caused a situation a lot like the "wild west," law and order have been unable to keep pace with societal sprawl into new territories. There may be a gold rush happening; there are also a lot of rattlesnakes and bandits as well.

ICOs

Initial coin offerings have grown in popularity as a crowdfunding form by basically allowing the recording and trading of ownership of stocks or shares, using a public, unforgeable, trustless, and encrypted blockchain.

The Digital Currency Index founder, Roger Bryan, said that he thinks more control will have to be made before cryptocurrency markets start to attract the type of institutional investments that a lot of these types of projects have to have for them to be able to reach their full potential.

At the moment, investors that are interested in staking a claim in the future of certain currencies using blockchain, token or project, can do this using the huge amounts of ICOs. This may also require a $10,000 or higher buy-in. On the other hand, if they want they can trade currencies, tokens, and coins, which are all called the collective name Cryptocurrency, on many different online exchanges.

Bitcoin tends to work like a "gatekeeper" of sorts; you typically need bitcoin to invest in different cryptocurrencies. This tends to be one of the most common uses for this particular currency and one that has most definitely played a large part in the continued rise in its value.

Bitcoin

A far as cryptocurrencies go, bitcoin is probably the most popular. Bitcoin contains its own market dynamics, community, and rule system. To get the most visible view of blockchains application is with bitcoin. Bitcoin has been in the news because it experiences rapid value gains. But there are also more than 2,000 other currencies and tokens that are based on distributed, cryptographical technology. There may be several other types of cryptocurrencies, but bitcoin is the most recognized name and has the biggest network and market float. Remember though that bitcoins "big" network is only relative. If compared to global money flows, it is barely a blip.

If you look at it in regions, though, you can find some evidence a lot of local use. An example would be that in some Latin American economies, they are using bitcoin as a solution for some of their economic and political instabilities. While looking at it this way, it does have some consumer benefit, as cryptocurrencies stand, they probably aren't going to go more mainstream because it does not have the same qualities of protection and consumer services like traditional financial institutions. Cryptocurrencies are an open road, but being the driver of your own finances and money, wouldn't be nice to have some guardrails?

Cryptocurrencies may have a long road ahead of them before they can reach mainstream, there are lots of great reasons to watch them and their evolution, and the evolution of the pattern that lies behind all cryptocurrencies: blockchain.

Blockchain

In recent years The Wall Street Journal has stated that more than 40 top financial institutions and several other companies over many different industries are looking at use cases of blockchain as a way to create a transparent and secure way for them to keep track of asset ownership digitally.

While blockchain is often called technology, it might be better to describe it as a design pattern. As I have described in earlier chapters, blockchain is basically a construct where a record of events is cryptographically authenticated and then distributed to various participants throughout a network and will be updated permanently after a consensus of the majority node ratifies the new entry. This type of design pattern can be applied and tweaked for solving lots of different challenges, but its main origins are powering different cryptocurrencies. Simply put, it is the working design that powers bitcoin and several other cryptocurrencies.

So is blockchain going to change how the banking world works completely? Probably not in the near future.

I think that blockchain has many years to go before it is retrofitted into the high-volume, and trusted global financial structure. As it sits right now, with the testing and implementation on any scale, it is an outlier that can be the solution for a certain trust problem for certain types of users. This type of specificity causes some issues in overhead computing, scale, settlement timing, and so on. Changing blockchain into a globally accepted and viable standard that works well with existing infrastructure for payments is pretty far into the future.

Since blockchain works like a design pattern that is cryptographically authenticated for the transfer of assets or values, there are several opportunities within the financial world where they could start implementing blockchain. If you look towards a bigger picture, the best frontier for the use of blockchain is automating the highly complex or manual financial products; this would include document-intensive processes. This would include everything from sealing a timestamp to securing credential viewership, automating mortgage papers, and providing notary services.

Cryptocurrency Clash

Different blockchain projects and coins stake claims in many different and unique selling points. Take Ripple as an example, they are targeted for use in the financial services industry, and to a certain extent, they have been implemented by global teams like UBS and Santander.

Another example currency is Dash, and they aim to beat out bitcoin by doing two things: providing more functions with smart contracts and increasing users' anonymity.

Another similar project is Ethereum, which has gained more attention from financial services and has yet another platform that can use smart contract and allow them to be executed and signed in an automated and decentralized way.

Many other coins have a niche or specialized application, such as online gambling tokens, are fairly popular along with currencies that are designed for trading across a large among of mobile and online games.

While it may be amazing to watch the twists and turns of the changing ecosystem of payments, the main thing is: as different payments start to become more popular and cash stays as the dominant form of payment, you have to understand and see that old payment options aren't being replaced; instead they are really coexisting. It's up to people like us to continue to help the consumer navigate the increasingly complex payment ecosystem as intuitively, seamlessly, and painlessly as possible.

How to Use Blockchain

While we have gone over what blockchain is and some of how to use it, I'm getting ready to take you more in depth. There may be some things in this chapter we have looked at earlier, but it's going to provide more information. First, we're going to look at how the bitcoin blockchain works through some decisions.

Data Storage

- Question: How should they store data?
- Bitcoin's answer: A blockchain
- Other ways: Use a database – could be repeated on many data centers

Data Distribution

- Question: How should they distribute new data?
- Bitcoin's answer: Peer-to-peer
- Other ways: Client-server, hierarchical

Consensus Mechanism

- Question: How can we resolve conflicts?
- Bitcoin's answer: Longest chain rule
- Other ways: Trusted or super-nodes

Upgrade Mechanism

- Question: How can the rules be changed?
- Bitcoin's answer: BIPs – writing rules, Vote with hashing power – implementing rules
- Other ways: contractual obligations, centralized upgrades

Participation Criteria

- Question: Who can submit a transaction?
- Bitcoin's answer: Pseudonymous, open
- Other ways: trusted, pre-vetted participants

Participation Criteria

- Question: Who can read data?
- Bitcoin's answer: Pseudonymous, open
- Other ways: trusted, pre-vetted participants

Participation Criteria

- Question: Who can validate transactions?
- Bitcoin's answer: Pseudonymous, open
- Other ways: trusted, pre-vetted participants

Participation Criteria

- Question: Who can add blocks?
- Bitcoin's answer: Pseudonymous, open
- Other ways: trusted, pre-vetted participants

Defense Mechanism

- Question: How to keep bad behavior away?
- Bitcoin's answer: Proof-of-work
- Other ways: Proof-of-stake, other proofs

Incentivisation Scheme

- Question: How can you incentivize block-makers?
- Bitcoin's answer: block reward, to be replaced by transaction fees
- Other ways: Contractual obligations, 3rd party funding

Incentivisation Scheme

- Question: How can you incentivize blockchain data storage?
- Bitcoin's answer: not considered
- Other ways: Contractual obligations, 3rd party funding

Incentivisation Scheme

- Question: How can you incentivize transaction validators?
- Bitcoin's answer: not considered
- Other ways: Contractual obligations, 3rd party funding

Blockchain Ordering

You've learned the basics of how a blockchain is made, and you know the basic parts of the blockchain. The blockchain is a file, and the file holds information, such as the content and header. Let's look at the ordering of a blockchain.

Page by page – When you are reading a book, the numerical page numbering makes it easy to know the page orders. If you take the pages out of a book and then shuffled them up, you could easily put them back in the order they are supposed to be so that they make sense.

Block by block – When it comes to blockchains, every block will reference the last block, not with just a number, but with a fingerprint of the block, which works better than just numbers because fingerprints are made up of the contents of a block.

Internal consistency – Since a fingerprint is used and not a numerical sequence or timestamp, you will also have a great way to validate the data. For any blockchain, you can make the fingerprints of a block by using algorithms. When fingerprints remain consistent with your information, and all of them make a chain, then you know that the internal workings of the blockchain are consistent. If people want to mess with your data, they will have to recreate every fingerprint from that stop on, and the new blockchain will look a bit different.

All of this means that if it's slow or difficult to make a fingerprint, then it will also be slow or difficult to re-write the blockchain.

Bitcoin's Logic

The logical reason as to why bitcoin made the blockchain work this way is:

- To make it harder to come up with a fingerprint that works with all the rules

- This means that if somebody wants to rewrite areas of the blockchain, it will take a lot longer, and they are going to have to get to and overtake the remaining honest network

These are the reasons why people claim that that bitcoin's blockchain is immutable, meaning that it is unable to be changed. But, in general, blockchains aren't really immutable. Also, when it comes to a peer-to-peer data sharing system, as well as the fingerprinting, will make it fairly obvious when somebody starts trying to alter the data if you do a good job of keeping up with the fingerprints.

Peer-to-peer is only one way that you can distribute date within a network. A second way is with a client-server. You are probably aware of the peer-to-peer file share that is used on BitTorrent network where they share files with users without using a central server that controls the data. This is the main reason behind BitTorrent's resiliency.

Client-server – In an office setting, data is often held within in many servers, and whatever computer you log in on, you can access this data. The server has 100% control of this data, and clients trust this as definitive data. The internet is made up of mostly client-server where sites are server controlled, and the client, you, can access it. This is the most traditional and efficient model of computing.

Peer-to-peer – With a peer-to-peer model, it works a lot like gossip where every peer controls all of the data or almost all of it, and everybody is given the updates. In some ways peer-to-peer tends to be not as efficient as a client-server because data can be replicated; once for every machine, and every change within the data causes a lot of new gossips. But, every peer is actually more independent and can operate to a certain extent if it were to lose connection with the remaining network. Peer-to-peer networks are typically bigger because there is not a central server that can be controlled, so getting rid of a peer-to-peer network takes a lot more work.

When it comes to a peer-to-peer network, even if all the peers involved are trusted, problems with consensus or agreements can come up. If every one of the peers is updating at a different speed and has a bit different state, how are they supposed to figure out which is the true or real state of the data?

With a peer-to-peer network that is untrusted, where you are unable to trust the other users, how do you make sure the system will not be corrupted easily by a bad user?

How to Resolve Conflicts?

An obvious conflict arises when several miners start to make blocks at about the same time. Since a block will take time to get to everybody in the network, which block should be considered legit?

Here is an example. Let's assume that every node in the network has synchronized their blockchains, and each one is a block number 80. If three miners make a block 81 at pretty much the same time, which one of these is going to be valid? Each one of the block 81s is going to appear to be a little bit different. They are going to all contain different payment addresses in the reward section, and they could have different transactions. For this example, they will be called 81a, 81b 81c.

How is this going to be resolved?

The longest chain rule. When using bitcoin, solve a conflict with the longest chain rule. With the example, it could be assumed that the first block 81 would be seen as valid. Pretend that 81a is the first new block you see. You could start to make another block on that one, creating 82a.

However, in the next few seconds, 81b might come along. After this shows up, you keep a watch on it. If 82b were to come along later and then according to the longest chain rule, this b chain would be considered the valid one: 80, 81b.

82b, and you would ignore all the short ones. You stop making 82a and start making an 83b.

This longest chain rule is what bitcoin's blockchains ecosystem uses to fix conflicts which comes up a lot in a distributed network. When it comes to a more trusted or centralized blockchain network, you can make decisions with the use of a senior or trusted validator to fix these cases.

As a whole network, you have to agree at the start about the data that is considered valid and is shared, and what is not. When it comes to bitcoin, they have technical rules for all of the transactions, such as filling in all the necessary data fields and using the correct format. They also have business rules, such as are you using more bitcoins that you actually have? Are those bitcoins being spent twice?

Rules change – When rules begin to change with time, how are the users in the network going to agree with the changes? Is there going to be a time where parts of the network will view the transaction as valid, while the others do not see it this way because of some logical difference?

With a controlled, private network, when one person has upgrade controls, it's simple to solve: "everybody has to upgrade to the new logic by 22 September." When it comes to an uncontrolled, public network, things start to become more challenging.

When it comes to bitcoin, each upgrade is made up of two parts:

1. BIPs, suggest the change

It starts with a proposal stage where somebody proposes the improvements, they are talked about and written out. This proposal is called a BIP, which stands for Bitcoin Improvement Proposal.

If this proposal were to be added to the software of bitcoin on Github, it would make up a part of the upgrade. This is in the new bitcoin core version where the most relevant "reference implementation" of the protocol lives.

1. Miners, start using the change

This upgrade can be downloaded by the nodes and the miners or block makers and then get used, but only if they are interested in it. You may think a change could reduce the reward for mining from 25 to 0.

If a network majority, with bitcoin this is determined through a computational power, decides to use the new version of the software, all of the new blocks will start to be made faster than blocks that use the old-style, and the people that are still using the old-style will eventually have to change or will become an unimportant fork in the blockchain. This means that miners that have a lot of computational power have a lot of control over the things that are implemented

Who Can Write Data?

When it comes to bitcoin, theoretically everybody can write or download software code, and then begin validating new transactions and make new blocks. All you have to do is go to bitcoin's website and run the core software.

Your computer is going to act just like a full node, meaning:

- Mining new blocks
- Making new blocks
- Passing valid blocks
- Validating blocks
- Listening for blocks

- Validating transactions
- Listening for transactions
- Storing a blockchain
- Downloading a blockchain
- Connecting with the bitcoin network

Bitcoin's core software source code is published on GitHub. If you want to, you can check out the code, compile it together, and then run it without having to download the prepackaged software on bitcoin.

Permissionless – Keep in mind that you do not have to sign up, login, or ask to be a part of this network. You are able just to jump right in and join. If you look at this alongside of a SWIFT network, in which you aren't able to just jump in and start listening in on the SWIFT messages. Because of this, there are some that like to call bitcoin "permissionless" VS SWIFT being "permissioned."

This does not mean that permissionless is the only way to go. You may be interested in using blockchain that is used in a private, trusted network. You may not be interested in having to publish all the rules that define what a valid block or transaction looks like. You may want to have some control over how the rules of a network are changed. Controlling a private, trusted network is often easier than a public, untrusted free-for-all like bitcoin.

How to Make Things Harder for Hackers?

One of the biggest problems with a permissionless or open network is that anybody can attack them. So you have to make sure that you can make the whole network as trustworthy as you can, even if specifics aren't.

What is a malicious attacker able and unable to do?

Dishonest miners can:

1. Refuse to send valid transaction information to another node.
2. Try and create a block that includes or does not include certain transactions that they choose.
3. Try and make a longer blockchain that will cause previously made blocks will end up as orphans and will no longer be part of the main chain.

The attacker is unable to:

1. Make new bitcoins out of thin air – note: an attacker's ledger can show "new" bitcoins, but all the other nodes are going to reject this, which is why you need to make sure that you verify a transaction through several nodes.
2. Steal your bitcoins
3. Pretend to be you or make payments on your behalf

When it comes to transactions, a dishonest miner has a very limited effect. If all the other people in the network are honest, they are going to reject all of the invalid transactions that the dishonest miners try to make, and they will be able to learn of the valid transaction from the trustworthy nodes, even if they will not pass on the info.

When it comes to blocks, if an attacker has a good amount of block creation power, and this is what controls everything, he can delay transactions by not including this information in their blocks. However, do not worry because your transaction will still be shared and know by all of the honest nodes, but it will be listed as an "unconfirmed transaction," and it will be included in their blocks.

The worst-case scenario of a malicious attacker will be if they make a longer blockchain than anybody else in the network has, and they use the "longest chain rule" to try and remove the honest shorter chains. This will give an attacker the power to unwind a transaction.

Here are some things that you can do to make it hard on hackers:

1. Make two payments the use the same bitcoins: one of them is sent to the online retailers, and the second is to yourself, which is an address that you control.
2. Make sure you only broadcast the payment the retailer receives.
3. When your payment is added to block that is honest, the retailer will then send you the goods.
4. Make a secret long chain of blocks that do not include the retailer payment, but house the payment that you made to yourself.
5. Publish this long chain. If the honest nodes us the "longest chain rule," then they will not pay attention to the honest blocks that have the retail payment on it and will build upon your chain. The honest block

will now be believed as orphaned and basically no longer exists.

6. Your original retailer payment will be seen as invalid by all of the honest nodes because the bitcoins are going to have already been spent.

This is what is referred to as a double spend since you are using same bitcoins twice, but the second amount are the ones that end up becoming a part of the blockchain, and the first will end up being rejected.

How are you able to make harder for the dishonest miners to make new blocks?

Keep in mind that this only becomes a problem for a ledger where there aren't any trusted block-makers.

Basically, you want to cause it be expensive or harder for an attacker to create blocks. With bitcoin, you do this by making it expensive computationally to create new blocks. By computationally expensive, I mean "requires a large amount of processing power," which is then translated to being financially expensive because a computer has to be bought and ran and maintained.

It's basically a guessing game when it comes to the computation where a block-maker has to guess a number. When this is worked in with the other block data, it will make a fingerprint/hash that is lower than the needed number. This is a number that coincides with the difficulty with mining, which also works with the networks total processing power. The higher number of computers that start to join in on processing blocks, the harder it will become for regulating a cycle.

This is called proof of work. When you publish a block that has a fingerprint smaller than the needed number, it shows that you did a good job at guessing to achieve what the network wanted.

How Are Validators Paid?

Block and transaction validation is fast and cheap unless you decide to cause it to be expensive and slow. If you are in control of the validators that are a part of your network, or if they are trusted, then:

- There is no need for you to make adding blocks expensive

- This means you can reduce the need for an incentive

You can also choose methods like saying, "people will sign contracts to run a validator and act honestly" or "we pay people who run validators."

Since Bitcoin has a public structure, it has to have a defense against attackers, so they use the proof of work system to make the computation harder to create new blocks. This has caused a bigger cost for mining, which means they have to use incentives for validators.

Similar to how gold prices will determine the amount you spend on equipment; bitcoin's price will determine how much power for mining will be used to make a network secure. The more the price is, the more mining that will happen, and an attacker will have to spend more to bully a network.

Miners will do quite a bit of mining the will increase the difficulty and rise walls up against an attacker. These people are then rewarded with bitcoins following a certain schedule, and over some time, as a block's reward goes down, transaction fees start to become the new incentive for miners.

It's helpful if you understand the workings of blockchain when it comes to bitcoin, but you shouldn't assume that all blockchain ecosystems have to have bitcoin mechanisms. Bitcoin was the first attempt at keeping up a decentralized, public ledger without any need for a formal governance or control. This means that there are going to be a lot of challenges

But, on the flip side, private blockchains and ledgers can be sent out to figure out other problems. Just like with everything there are going to be the good side and the bad side with every type of solution, and you need to consider all of them individually.

Pros and Cons

From all the information I've provided about blockchain, you can see that blockchain provides a lot of advantages. As with anything, there is going to be some downsides to blockchain. Let's look at some of the pros and cons of blockchain.

Pros

1. Maintain contracts

The blockchain is instrumental for storing digital contracts that allows automatic releases of payments to the supplier and shipper.

1. Disintermediation and trustless exchange

Blockchain lets people make exchanges without needing a middleman. It allows an exchange to take place and reduces and possibly eliminates any risk that is associated with third parties.

1. Faster transactions

When making a transaction through a bank, it can take about three to five business days to process. If you need to make a transaction near the weekend, this will add two more days to the process. By using blockchain, transaction times get reduced to minutes instead of days and can be done at any time, 24/7.

1. Serves as an unlimited registry

Blockchain provides a registry for ownership information and maintenance status for everything that is on the internet.

1. Transparency and immutability

If changes are made to blockchains that are public, everyone can see what the changes were. They are immutable. This means that they cannot be altered or deleted.

1. Empowered users

Every user has complete control of their information and transactions.

1. Preserving intellectual property

Individuals used to have to go through third parties to package and distribute their goods. They would have to pay a percentage to this company. By using blockchain, they can create a startup and registries and get the full payment for their work.

1. Giving processes more integrity

Users know that their transactions will be done just like the rules state, this removes any necessity for third parties.

1. High-quality data

All data that is contained in a blockchain is complete, accurate, timely, widely available, and consistent.

1. Transaction costs are lowered

Because using blockchain gets rid of needing third parties and overhead costs during the exchange of assets, this reduces the transaction fees by a lot.

1. Longevity, durability, and reliability

Because blockchain is a decentralized network, it takes away the central point failing. This makes it possible to stop attacks.

1. Ecosystem simplification

Every transaction is put into a public ledger. This reduces any chaos or problems that might arise with multiple ledgers.

The benefits of using blockchain can be seen in many different businesses.

- Healthcare

Using blockchain to get digital signatures that can only allow access if authorized by many people. This helps to regulate the availability and the privacy of a person's health records. It can group the entire community like patients, hospitals, insurance companies, and doctors. This could reduce healthcare fraud.

- Defense

People need the ability to keep important defense infrastructures such as operating systems and network firmware safe from unauthorized access or modifications. If any unauthorized access happened, it might cause serious compromises to the national security. The blockchain is spread across many different data centers that will make sure security is in place for attacks within the important networks.

- Government

Blockchain allows groups to work together to meet common goals. In one entity, there are bosses and the normal hierarchy that mandates one single source of truth. When entities interact, there must be something in place to help with conflict resolution. For blockchains to add value, they must be used in collaboration across the workflow.

It helps to protect entities within a nation if it gets used correctly. If banks can share data without revealing the data to each other, double invoicing could be avoided. You would be able to access the invoice that was issued on blockchain and signed, and the digital record cannot be copied or financed more than one time.

Singapore wants to build a smart nation. Blockchains can replace centralized ledgers with decentralized ones. They could lead the way in making trust, tamperproof repositories. Assets, property, registries, national identity, and insurance can all be stored in blockchains. This allows for easier verification. This could reduce settlement times when there is an ownership change. With smart contracts, automated title transfers could happen when certain information is met.

- Law

Blockchains can hold a lot of data, and this includes contracts. Smart contracts or contracts that are made using blockchain can eliminate the need for a third party, in this instance a legal firm. It will allow payments to be made based on what milestone is being met.

- Energy

Microgeneration in electricity has become common in the power business. Solar power and home power generation are closing the gap between power supply around the whole world. As microgeneration grows, it begins to make an energy market. Smart meters can register consumed and produced electricity in a blockchain. This makes it possible to use surplus energy in different locations.

Cons

Here are the larger known downsides of blockchain:

1. Lack of privacy

Transparency, which is normally looked at as being a good thing might not be for everyone. Blockchain's transparency lets everyone see every one of your transactions.

1. Uncertain regulatory status

Modern currencies have been controlled and created by national governments. Blockchain and bitcoin face problems with widespread acceptance by established financial institutions if the government regulation stays irregular.

1. Not enough proven case studies

There is plenty of proof that blockchain could improve currency exchange, but there is not much proof about the use of blockchain with other applications. People just assume blockchain can improve things, but there just is not enough proof that shows it will.

1. Nascent technology.

Blockchain must resolve some challenges with their verification process, transaction speed, and data limits so they can gain worldwide applicability.

1. Cost

Even though blockchain can offer savings in time and cost transactions, it has a high initial capital cost that deters some users.

1. Integration concerns

To use blockchain, you must make major changes, or total replacement, of your current system. Companies must be sure they strategize the transition.

1. Large energy consumption

Uses will use a huge amount of computer power when doing transactions. With a bitcoin blockchain, network mines are trying to do 450 thousand trillion solutions each second.

1. Adopted cultures

The blockchain is a complete change from a decentralized network where users must buy-in.

1. Security, control, and privacy

Even though blockchains have strong encryption and private blockchains, there are still many cybersecurity problems that need to be handled before everybody will trust giving out their personal details to a blockchain.

Most people say that there are more pros for blockchains when compared to the cons. Taking your needs into consideration is important. The odds of blockchain getting used worldwide for everything are slim to none. It is a great alternative to the technology that is in place right now.

Conclusion

Thank for making it through to the end of Blockchain. I hope it was informative and able to provide you with all of the tools you need to achieve your goals of learning more about how blockchain works and the benefits it can have in various areas of your life.

The next step is to think about how you can use blockchain in your life. As you've learned, it can be helpful in many areas, not just cryptocurrency. If you have an e-commerce business, it's a great security measure. Looking further into learning about their smart contracts may also be good for you.

Finally, if you found this book useful in any way, a review on Amazon is always appreciated!

www.ingramcontent.com/pod-product-compliance
Lightning Source LLC
Chambersburg PA
CBHW050014230526
45470CB00003B/959